NORTH AMERICAN ANIMALS

Rocky Mountain Elk

by Rebecca Sabelko

BELLWETHER MEDIA · MINNEAPOLIS, MN

Note to Librarians, Teachers, and Parents:

Blastoff! Readers are carefully developed by literacy experts and combine standards-based content with developmentally appropriate text.

Level 1 provides the most support through repetition of high-frequency words, light text, predictable sentence patterns, and strong visual support.

Level 2 offers early readers a bit more challenge through varied simple sentences, increased text load, and less repetition of high-frequency words.

Level 3 advances early-fluent readers toward fluency through increased text and concept load, less reliance on visuals, longer sentences, and more literary language.

Level 4 builds reading stamina by providing more text per page, increased use of punctuation, greater variation in sentence patterns, and increasingly challenging vocabulary.

Level 5 encourages children to move from "learning to read" to "reading to learn" by providing even more text, varied writing styles, and less familiar topics.

Whichever book is right for your reader, Blastoff! Readers are the perfect books to build confidence and encourage a love of reading that will last a lifetime!

This edition first published in 2019 by Bellwether Media, Inc.

No part of this publication may be reproduced in whole or in part without written permission of the publisher. For information regarding permission, write to Bellwether Media, Inc., Attention: Permissions Department, 6012 Blue Circle Drive, Minnetonka, MN 55343.

Library of Congress Cataloging-in-Publication Data

Names: Sabelko, Rebecca, author.
Title: Rocky Mountain Elk / by Rebecca Sabelko.
Description: Minneapolis, MN : Bellwether Media, Inc., 2019. | Series:
   Blastoff! Readers. North American Animals | Audience: Age 5-8. | Audience:
   Grade K to 3. | Includes bibliographical references and index.
Identifiers: LCCN 2017056264 (print) | LCCN 2018005320 (ebook) | ISBN
   9781626178007 (hardcover : alk. paper) | ISBN 9781681035253 (ebook)
Subjects: LCSH: Rocky Mountain elk–North America–Juvenile literature.
Classification: LCC QL737.U55 (ebook) | LCC QL737.U55 S2175 2019 (print) |
   DDC 599.65/7–dc23
LC record available at https://lccn.loc.gov/2017056264

Editor: Betsy Rathburn   Designer: Josh Brink

Printed in the United States of America, North Mankato, MN.

Table of Contents

Rocky Mountain elk are large members of the deer family. These **mammals** once roamed much of North America.

4

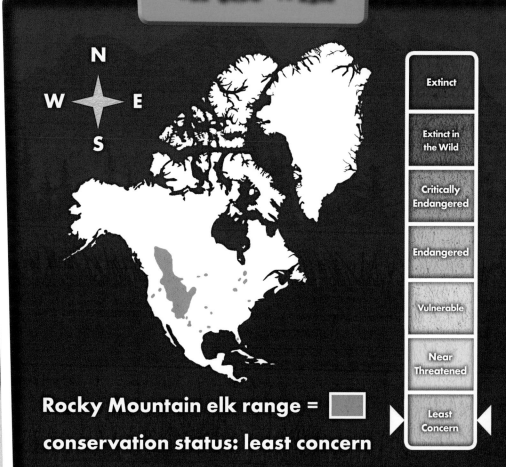

In the Wild

N
W E
S

Extinct

Extinct in the Wild

Critically Endangered

Endangered

Vulnerable

Near Threatened

Least Concern

Rocky Mountain elk range = ▢

conservation status: least concern

Today, their range is smaller.
They live in the Rocky Mountains
of Canada and the United States.
Small **herds** also live outside
the mountains.

These elk live in **alpine meadows**, dry desert valleys, and hardwood forests.

Rocky Mountain elk often **migrate** with the seasons. Summers may be spent high in the mountains. In winter, they find food at the bases of mountains.

calves

Rocky Mountain elk are social mammals. Herds of females and their **calves** stick together year-round.

Males live either alone or in small groups for most of the year. In the fall, they gather **harems** of females.

rump patch

Rocky Mountain elk can weigh 700 pounds (315 kilograms) and stand over 5 feet (1.5 meters) tall!

Size of a Rocky Mountain Elk

Rocky Mountain elk

average human

6
5
4
3
2
1
(feet)

In warmer months, these elk have reddish brown hair. It lightens in winter. Light **rump patches** are easy to spot all year.

velvet

Males **shed** and grow new **antlers** each year. During late spring and summer, **velvet** covers the antlers while they grow.

Identify a Rocky Mountain Elk

rump patch   branched antlers   throat mane

The velvet peels away by late September. Then, the antlers are fully grown!

Rocky Mountain Elk are **herbivores**. They mostly eat different types of grasses.

alpine bluegrass

prairie junegrass

green needlegrass

elk thistle

juniper

huckleberries

Grasses are harder to find during winter. The elk eat other plants like shrubs, tree bark, and twigs.

These elk do not have many **predators**. Mountain lions and gray wolves are their main enemies.

Rocky Mountain elk bark to warn each other of danger. Large herd sizes also keep them safe.

Spotted Calves

Throughout late spring, females give birth to one or two calves. The calves have white spots and no scent. Calves spend their first weeks alone with their mothers. Then, they join the harem.

Baby Facts

Name for babies:	calves
Size of litter:	1 or 2 calves
Length of pregnancy:	about 255 days
Time spent with mom:	about 1 year

Calves **nurse** through fall.
They begin to eat grasses, too.

They spend a year with their mothers. Once new calves arrive, the **yearlings** are ready to care for themselves!

Glossary

alpine meadows—grassy fields that are found high up in mountains

antlers—branched bones on the heads of some animals; antlers look like horns.

calves—baby Rocky Mountain elk

harems—groups of female Rocky Mountain elk controlled by one male

herbivores—animals that only eat plants

herds—groups of Rocky Mountain elk that live and travel together

mammals—warm-blooded animals that have backbones and feed their young milk

migrate—to travel from one place to another, often with the seasons

nurse—to drink mom's milk

predators—animals that hunt other animals for food

rump patches—the area of light-colored fur around the rumps of Rocky Mountain elk

shed—to lose something on the body at the same time every year; Rocky Mountain elk shed their antlers.

velvet—the fuzzy skin that covers a bull's antlers

yearlings—Rocky Mountain elk that are one year old

To Learn More

AT THE LIBRARY
Borgert-Spaniol, Megan. *Caribou*. Minneapolis, Minn.: Bellwether Media, 2018.

Meinking, Mary. *Wolf vs. Elk*. Chicago, Ill.: Raintree, 2011.

Poppele, Jonathan. *Animal Tracks of the Rocky Mountains*. Cambridge, Minn.: Adventure Publications, Inc., 2017.

ON THE WEB
Learning more about Rocky Mountain elk is as easy as 1, 2, 3.

1. Go to www.factsurfer.com.

2. Enter "Rocky Mountain elk" into the search box.

3. Click the "Surf" button and you will see a list of related web sites.

With factsurfer.com, finding more information is just a click away.

Index